YOU CHOOSE
BOOKS
CAN YOU
VIRUS OU ?
An Interactive Doomsday Adventure
by MATT DOEDEN
illustrated by STEWART JOHNSON
CAPSTONE PRESS
a capstone imprint

You Choose Books are published by Capstone Press,
1710 Roe Crest Drive, North Mankato, Minnesota 56003
www.capstonepub.com

Library of Congress Cataloging-in-Publication Data
Doeden, Matt, author.
  Can you survive a virus outbreak? : an interactive doomsday adventure /
by Matt Doeden.
       pages cm.—(You choose books. You choose : doomsday)
  Summary: "A You Choose adventure about surviving a virus outbreak"—Provided
by publisher.
  Audience: Ages 8–12
  Audience: Grades 4 to 6
  Includes bibliographical references and index.
  ISBN 978-1-4914-5851-8 (library binding)
  ISBN 978-1-4914-5924-9 (paperback)
  ISBN 978-1-4914-5936-2 (ebook pdf)
1. Epidemics—Juvenile literature. 2. Communicable diseases—Juvenile literature.
3. Survival—Juvenile literature. 4. Plot-your-own stories. I. Title.
  RA653.5.D64 2016
  614.4—dc23   2015002014

Editorial Credits
Anthony Wacholtz, editor; Bobbie Nuytten, designer; Wanda Winch,
media researcher; Kathy McColley, production specialist;
Nathan Gassman, creative director

Photo Credits
Getty Images: DEA/De Agostini/G. DAGLI ORTI, 102; Shutterstock: AlexVector,
background (throughout), Ihor Pasternak, 107 (left), Irina_QQQ, design element,
Mtsaride, 107 (right), tomwa, 106, tuulijumala, 111

Printed in Canada.
032015   008825FRF15

TABLE OF CONTENTS

ABOUT YOUR
ADVENTURE

YOU are living through a dark and dangerous time in the near future of humanity. A terrible new virus is about to wreak havoc on the world's population. How will you survive? Start off by turning the page, then follow the directions at the bottom of each page. The choices you make will change your outcome. After you finish your path, go back and read the others to see how other choices would have changed your fate. Do you have what it takes to survive doomsday?

YOU CHOOSE the path you take through a Virus Outbreak.

BLOOD FEVER

You can barely contain your excitement as you gaze out the window of your airplane seat. You fidget in your seat, eager for the flight to reach its destination, Port au Prince, Haiti. You smirk, knowing your classmates are back home, sitting in algebra class right now. But you're getting a head start on spring break—a two-week visit to Haiti to visit your sister Tara. She's a medical student, volunteering in a small village in the poverty-stricken nation of Haiti.

After you land, you check your phone. There's a text from Tara: *Running late. Sry!*

Great, you think with a groan. You find a comfortable seat and watch people come and go. It's a bustling airport. People are scrambling in line at the ticketing booths.

Turn the page

A man in a suit and tie sitting next to you is reading the sports section of a newspaper. The front page sits on the open seat between you.

"Mind if I read this?" you ask.

He shrugs and hands you the paper. "Be my guest. But there's not much in here for a kid. Terrorist attacks in South Asia, stock market crashing, a nasty virus spreading outside Santo Domingo. Adult stuff. Might be a crossword puzzle in the back, though."

You mutter a "thank you" and try not to roll your eyes. You may still be a kid, but that doesn't mean you're not interested in current events. You glance at every story. The outbreak in Santo Domingo—the media is calling it Blood Fever—catches your attention. Santo Domingo is the capital of the Dominican Republic, a nation that shares the island of Hispaniola with Haiti. Nobody seems to know where the outbreak came from. Scary stuff, but you're sure that doctors will get it under control. After all, this is the 21st century.

An hour passes, then two. Suddenly you notice that the lines for customs are empty. People coming and going seem agitated. Several airport employees rush by, speaking loudly.

"Parlez-vous anglais?" you ask a woman at a help desk. You're in French class at school, but you're not ready for a full conversation with a native speaker.

"Oui," she answers. "I speak English."

"What's going on?" you ask.

"It's Blood Fever. They've found some cases here in Haiti."

Before you can reply, you hear someone calling your name. It's Tara! She rushes over and wraps you up in a giant hug.

"So sorry to be late," Tara says. "One of my patients took a bad turn. Had to get her stable before I left."

"It's not Blood Fever, is it?" you ask nervously.

"No, no. It couldn't be. Probably just a flu bug."

Turn the page

"They say that the virus has spread to Haiti," you tell Tara.

"Really? News travels slowly out here, but that's surprising. We knew it would spread. But so quickly?"

Over Tara's shoulder, you see lines at the ticketing booth growing. People are pushing and shoving, trying to move to the front.

"Maybe your being here isn't such a good idea," Tara says. "We should put you on a flight home."

Your heart sinks. You've been looking forward to this trip for months.

"You're staying, right?" you ask.

"Of course. If there's an outbreak, they'll need all the help they can get."

Going home would probably be the wise decision. But you can't bear the thought of turning around and getting right back on a plane.

To stay with Tara, go to page 11.
To get in line to buy a ticket home, turn to page 61.

"If you're staying, I'm staying," you tell Tara, tossing your backpack over your shoulder.

"All right then," she says. "Let's get going. We've got a two-hour drive ahead of us."

You climb into Tara's small rental car. You leave the sprawling terraces of Port au Prince behind and trace the coast along the highway. Soon you turn north onto a small dirt road, rumbling up steep terrain to a little village.

"That's where we're working," Tara says, pointing to a small group of tents. "We live in a small barracks on the other side of the village. Mainly we vaccinate kids against diseases—measles, whooping cough, the usual suspects. But we also help with locals who need care."

Tara parks the car and leads you through the village. The homes are run-down, and animals roam through the streets. But the people are warm. They greet you as you pass by, offering smiles and waves.

Turn the page

"Here we are," she says, gesturing you into the crude field hospital they've set up. "I'll get you settled into your barrack in a moment. Just want to check on Maria first. She's the patient I was seeing earlier."

Several people lie on cots. One has a broken arm. Another is bent over with a rattling cough. Maria is in the back, separated from the rest with plastic sheets. You watch from outside as Tara steps in and slips on gloves and a mask. Maria is a young woman, maybe 25 years old. Her skin is pale and waxy, and she seems barely conscious. Tara rests her hand on Maria's forehead and frowns.

"She's burning up," Tara tells Jim, one of the other medical students.

"I know," he says. "We can't seem to control the fever. And it gets worse." Jim lifts the sheet and points to a bright red rash of tiny blood blisters covering Maria's chest and shoulders.

Tara flinches. "How ... it can't be here already."

Turn the page

Jim shakes his head. "I don't get it either. But there's no doubt. Blood Fever is here, and we're not ready for it. No one is."

Tara spends several more minutes talking with Jim. Then she peels off her gloves and mask and joins you outside. "Look," she says. "I'm not sure having you here is a great idea. I didn't know the virus would be here so soon. Maybe it's best if you keep your distance."

"Please," you beg. "I want to help. It's why I came!"

Tara sighs. She's never been able to say no to you. "Okay, look. If you come back to the hospital with me, you wear gloves and a mask at all times. And no direct contact with patients. Or ... I have another way you can help. Jim has been studying the local herbs here. You could go out and collect some that have immune-boosting properties. They might just give us an edge against this virus."

To return to the hospital with Tara, go to page 15.
To talk to Jim and gather herbs, turn to page 16.

"I want to see you in action," you tell Tara.

Tara grins. "Okay, then," she says, handing you a surgical mask. "First thing, any time you're even near the hospital, wear this mask. The virus is super contagious."

After a quick tour of the hospital, Tara puts you to work. It's not quite what you imagined. Instead of drawing blood or taking temperatures, you're fetching food and water, cleaning bedsheets, and setting up cots.

The cases start as a trickle. But soon they come more rapidly. After two days you have six cases. After three, the number swells to 17. Maria drifts in and out of consciousness. She doesn't seem to be improving.

The next day, Jim speaks up over breakfast. "It's getting worse," he says. "The hospitals in Port au Prince are overrun. There are dead in the streets, and the airport is closed. Before things get worse, we need supplies. Today might be our last chance if things continue to fall apart."

To go to Port au Prince with Jim, turn to page 18.
To stay back and help with the patients, turn to page 25.

You catch Jim just as he's leaving the hospital. He looks exhausted. "Two more cases came in last night, and Maria is growing worse by the hour," he tells you as you walk together. "It's spreading much faster than anyone expected. Things are going to get really bad around here. It might be time for you to get out."

"Nah," you tell him with a grin. "I want to help. Tara thought you might put me to work by gathering herbs."

"The locals swear by them," Jim says. "There's an old woman a few villages north who can name every plant that grows here. I spent a few days with her, learned some things. I'm not sure how much herbs really help, but we've got precious little medicine here. It's better than nothing."

You walk together as Jim tells you what to look for. Sarsaparilla root … mint leaves … bitterwood bark … the list goes on. He grabs a book from his bunk. It's loaded with photos of native plants. "Find what you can," Jim says.

You head northeast of the village. You spend your day creeping through forests, scrambling up rocks, and digging out roots. Before you realize how late it's gotten, the sun is setting. You better get back while you've still got some light. Grasping your bag loaded with leaves, bark, and roots, you turn to head back.

You take a sharp breath and swallow a scream. Someone is watching you! The figure is cloaked in robes and appears stooped over. Your heart races.

To turn and run, turn to page 20.
To approach the stranger, turn to page 22.

The rusty old Jeep rumbles down the highway. The road is almost deserted. In the distance, you see smoke rising above the trees. You don't want to know what's burning.

The smell hits you as you arrive at the outer limits of the city. It instantly takes you back to the day when you found a dead raccoon in your basement.

"There's a supermarket a few blocks ahead," he says, turning the Jeep down a side street. A thin man waves at you from the other side of the street, and starts stumbling in your direction. He shouts to you in a raspy voice. The man's face is flushed and marked with small blisters.

"He's asking us for help," Jim says, shaking his head. "But he's sick. There's no telling what he might do."

The man continues to shout to you urgently. He seems desperate.

To let the man approach, turn to page 29.
To ask Jim to get you out of there, turn to page 32.

As fast as you can, you turn and dart off into the woods. You run, tree branches slapping your face, until your foot slips on a loose rock. Your ankle twists, and you shout out as you crumple to the ground. Your bag of herbs sprawls out before you, its contents spread across the ground.

Your ankle throbs, but it's not broken. You look around as you catch your breath. There's nobody else here. But you don't recognize the landscape. You're at the base of a rocky hill. The sun is almost completely down. Quickly, you get your bearings. "West is that way," you mumble to yourself.

There's not much light left, and you'll be limping, so time is critical. You grab a few of the herbs lying nearby, but end up leaving most of them where they lie. You know as long as you move west, you'll hit the little dirt road that leads to the village.

As you limp along, the sky grows dark. As the air cools, a swarm of mosquitoes buzz around you. You swat and slap as you move, but the bugs are relentless. By the time you find the dirt road and follow it back to the village, you're covered in itchy bites.

"Thank goodness!" Tara cries as you limp into town. "What happened to you?"

Others gather around as you tell your tale. You notice Jim smirking in the background.

"That sounds like Leila," Jim says. "She's the woman I was telling you about. The locals call her a leaf doctor. She was probably gathering herbs, like you were."

You groan, feeling silly for running away from an old woman. "I'll go back out tomorrow," you tell Jim. "Now I know what I'm looking for."

You have a restless night, itching at all of your bug bites. You roll out of bed at sunrise, but you feel terrible. Your stomach is churning, and you're sweating.

To report to the hospital, turn to page 34.
To head out to collect herbs, turn to page 39.

"Bonjour," you say, stepping forward. "Hello?"

The stranger straightens and peels back a hood. It's an old woman. A pack is slung over her shoulder. She smiles at you.

She doesn't speak English, but your French is just good enough to keep a conversation going. Her name is Leila, and she's gathering herbs, just like you are. It doesn't take long before you realize she's the woman Jim told you about—a "leaf doctor."

She waves you over with her hand. She wants you to come with her. You look back toward the village and see the sun is already beginning to set. Tara will be worried, but you feel like you should go with her.

You spend the night in Leila's small hut. It's an amazing experience. Carefully, step-by-step, Leila shows you how to make a tea from nearly a dozen local herbs. She boils water in a small pot, carefully adding herbs as she goes. Finally, she hands you a steaming cup.

Turn the page

You drink it. It's bitter, but you swallow down every last drop. Leila smiles and pats your head.

In the morning, you head back. Your pack is loaded with all of the herbs you need to make Leila's tea. You follow the small dirt road southwest. The hike takes more than an hour, but you feel energized.

Tara rushes up and wraps you in a bear hug as you enter the village. "Don't ever do that again!" she scolds.

You tell everyone your tale and show them the herbs Leila gave you. "There's not a sick person in her whole village," you explain. Some of the med students seem skeptical. You know many doctors have a low opinion of herbal treatments. "What harm is there in trying?" you ask.

Soon you're at work brewing Leila's tea, carefully following the steps she taught you. You've got enough for about 20 people. But who would benefit most from drinking it, the healthy or the sick?

To give the tea to the med students and other healthy people in the village, turn to page 43.
To give the tea to the sick patients, turn to page 47.

The hospital is filling at an alarming rate. Your day is filled with washing soiled bedsheets, carrying water from the well to the hospital, and doing anything you can to be useful. The work is hard, and by evening you're exhausted. But it feels good to make a difference.

As the sun sets, that feeling quickly fades. Jim hasn't returned from his supply run. "It's not like him," Tara says, wringing her hands. "I can't imagine he would have just abandoned us."

You're not sure what to say. Jim could be in trouble. His Jeep could have broken down. He could have gotten sick—or worse.

Turn the page

"I feel like I should go after him," Tara says. "One of the villagers has a motorcycle that I'm sure I could use. But with Jim gone, they can't spare any help at the hospital. We're getting more and more patients, and the fever is already more than we can handle."

She's distraught. You have a feeling that you're never going to see Jim again, one way or the other. But you hate seeing Tara like this. Maybe you could give her some peace of mind by looking for Jim yourself. The village can do without you for a day, but the people need Tara.

To convince Tara you are both needed at the hospital, turn to page 28.
To volunteer to take the motorcycle into Port au Prince to look for Jim, turn to page 58.

"If he's gone, he's gone," you tell Tara with a hug. "Even if you know where he was going, the odds of finding him are pretty low. We just have to wait. In the meantime, we can try to help these people."

Tara sighs with tears in her eyes. She knows you're right. The days stretch on, and the sick continue to come in. There's been no sign of Jim. You hope he found a safe place, even if you don't really believe it.

Within a week, the hospital is overflowing. You wash your hands several times every hour and wear a mask and gloves. You minimize close contact with everyone—including Tara. But it's not enough. Just 10 days after you arrived in Haiti, you wake up in the morning feeling ill. You rush outside and vomit, followed by 10 minutes of painful dry heaves.

You close your eyes and rest for a moment. You try to convince yourself it's just the flu or something you ate. But you recognize the symptoms of Blood Fever. It's time to break the bad news to Tara.

Turn to page 50.

"The whole reason we came to Haiti was to help, wasn't it?" you say before Jim can drive away. He closes his eyes and slumps his shoulders.

"Yeah, you're right. Okay, let's do what we can."

The sick man appears to be in his 30s, but the fever has hit him hard. His skin sags off his arms and dark circles hang under his eyes. His half-panicked speech is too rapid for you to follow, but Jim is fluent in French. They speak for several moments before Jim turns to you.

"His wife has died, and his child is sick. He's begging for us to help him."

You both agree you'll do what you can. The man leads you to his nearby home—a small shack with a dirt floor. You enter and wince. The smell of death here is overwhelming.

Turn the page

The child—a young boy, perhaps 4 years old—lies on a pile of blankets on the floor. Jim places his hand on the child's forehead. "He's burning up," he whispers. "His fever is advanced. There's nothing we can do."

As the three of you stand over the boy, the father begins to hack and cough. When he pulls his hand away from his mouth, it's covered in blood and mucus. You feel helpless.

Jim reaches into his backpack. He pulls out a water bottle, presses it into the man's hand, and walks back outside. You follow him out.

"They're dying and you give them water?"

Jim shrugs. "What else could I do? They're both desperately dehydrated. I told him that it was medicine. And that's as close to the truth as there is."

"Do we go to the market then?"

"No," Jim says, shaking his head. "There's nothing there. He told me that everything's been cleaned out for days."

It's a somber ride back to the village. The sun is setting as you pull in. Tara rushes out and wraps you up in a big hug. "I was so worried," she says. There's a tear on her cheek.

As bad as things seem, they only get worse. Two patients died while you were away. The next day, three more join them. You help Jim and some others dig graves. By the end of the day, you're completely exhausted and drenched in sweat. You sit down for some supper with the rest, but you just can't bring yourself to eat anything.

That night, you can't sleep. Your stomach roils and grumbles. Around midnight, you step outside and vomit violently onto the ground. You lie there a moment, shivering, knowing what this means. You're sick. And there's no cure.

Turn to page 50.

As the man draws near, it becomes clear that he's in an advanced state of infection. Before he can reach your Jeep, he doubles over in a fit of coughing. His hands are covered in blood. He's well beyond your help.

"Go," you say quietly. "We can't help him, Jim. We have to go."

The man slumps to the road as you drive off. Your heart sinks as you watch him collapse. But you had no choice.

Several blocks down the road, you arrive at your destination. Jim curses as he surveys the scene. The doors have been torn off the hinges. Broken shelves and shredded food packaging litters the parking lot. Several young men stand near the entrance, fixing very hard gazes on the two of you.

"It might not be empty," Jim says. But neither of you really believe it.

"We gotta go, Jim." The young men standing by the door have started to move in your direction. They do not look friendly. "Jim … now, Jim!"

Finally, with a disgusted shake of his head, Jim puts the Jeep in gear and slams the accelerator. That's when you hear the shot ring out. The Jeep lurches violently to one side. "The tires!" Jim shouts. "They're shooting at the tires!"

Another shot rings out, and the Jeep grinds to a halt. A look over your shoulder sends a chill down your spine. They're coming for you.

"Stay calm," Jim says. "They probably only want our money and supplies."

He steps out of the Jeep, his hands in the air. Your heart is racing. The young men approaching look desperate and very threatening. You rest your hand on the door handle.

To open the door and run, turn to page 52.
To stay in the Jeep and let Jim talk to them,
turn to page 56.

Something's not right. You need to see Tara or one of the other med students right away. You wipe the sweat off your brow and limp down to the hospital. But as you approach, a chill runs down your spine. Jim and another med student are carrying a stretcher. On it rests a slender figure, wrapped in a bedsheet. You don't have to ask. You already know—it's Maria.

Tara rushes out of the hospital and wraps you in an embrace. You hold your breath—if you've got Blood Fever, you don't want to infect Tara. "Oh, we tried," Tara says, weeping. "There just wasn't anything we could do. And the others are getting worse so quickly. There's more than a dozen now. More coming in every hour, it seems."

Turn the page

You hate to tell her, but you have no choice. You push out of her hug and take a step back. "Tara … you need to wear your mask."

"I don't understand," she says. But you can see in her face that she does. "Oh no … not you! Maybe it's something else. Something you ate."

"Maybe," you say, nodding. "But maybe not."

It doesn't take long to find out. Tara takes some blood and runs a test. It's official. You've got Blood Fever. You overhear one of the other med students talking about the disease spreading through mosquito bites. That must be how the disease found you.

Tara is determined to get you to a proper hospital. She begs Jim to take you into Port au Prince. Reluctantly, he agrees. Within an hour, the three of you are in Jim's Jeep, rumbling down the road. The bumpy motion of the Jeep makes you feel ill. You make Jim pull over so you can vomit into a ditch.

"You're not looking so hot," Jim says. You know it's true. One moment, you're burning up. The next, you've got the chills. It's a long, miserable ride. And your mood doesn't improve when you reach the city.

Port au Prince has been hit hard. Fires burn in the distance. People lie sleeping in the streets. At least you hope they're sleeping. Jim weaves through the streets of the city, finally pulling up to a large, gated building. The sign reads "Hôpital Asile Français D'Haiti." Jim tells you to wait and goes inside.

Twenty minutes later, he returns to the Jeep. He slams the door shut in disgust. "They're not admitting anyone," he says. "Every bed is filled. They don't have the staff."

Turn the page

You try several other hospitals in the city, but the story is always the same. Blood Fever has overwhelmed them. And now doctors and nurses are starting to get sick. There's simply nowhere to turn.

By the time the three of you return to the village, it's dark. You're exhausted and weak. It takes both Jim and Tara to help you to your bed. You notice Tara's face streaked with tears.

The virus hits you harder than most. Within a day, you're covered in painful blood blisters. You can't keep food or water down. Tara does all she can, but she never has a chance. Just eight days after your first symptom, your fever soars to 106 degrees. It's more than your body can take. You slip away into a deep darkness, one victim among millions of the terrible Blood Fever.

THE END
To follow another path, turn to page 10.
To learn more about virus outbreaks, turn to page 103.

You're determined to bring Jim the herbs he asked for. Maybe some fresh morning air will help you feel better. You take off north of the village, keeping a sharp eye for what you need. Now that you've done this once before, you're confident you can get what you need and be back before the day gets too hot.

You've barely walked half a mile before you have to stop to rest. Sweat pours down your face, and you feel your knees trembling. You drink deeply from your canteen of water, but moments later, your stomach heaves. You retch and throw it all back up.

Turn the page

Uh-oh, you think. You're beginning to realize that you're truly ill. Last night you were feeling fine, and now you can barely make yourself move. How could you have gotten sick so fast?

You scratch one of your mosquito bites and your fingers come away bloody. You stare at the smear of red, and it hits you. The mosquitoes! That's how Blood Fever is spreading so quickly. The mosquitoes are carrying it! And you were bitten dozens of times. You've got to tell Tara. Maybe this information will be useful. They could set up mosquito nets ... get bug spray ... *something*!

You stand and begin to march back to the village. But your head is swimming. Was it this way? You shake your head, trying to clear the cobwebs. No ... it's that way. No ...

Turn the page

Just standing has you feeling lightheaded. Black begins to creep in around the edges of your vision. The next thing you know, you're lying on the ground. You fainted. Your head is aching. You must have hit it on a rock. Now blood is pooling on the ground below you. Once again you retch and heave.

"Help!" you shout, but it's a feeble yell, and you're far from the village. You're dehydrated, and it's getting worse by the moment as you bleed. You can't stand without passing out, and no help is coming. You know it's a bad idea, but all you want to do is close your eyes. You fight the urge for a few moments, but it's pointless. You quickly drift off to a sleep from which you won't awaken.

THE END

To follow another path, turn to page 10.
To learn more about virus outbreaks, turn to page 103.

Your first instinct is to give Leila's tea to the sick. But the more you think about it, the more you're convinced it's the healthy who would benefit most. The herbs are supposed to boost the immune system. That might keep people from catching the virus in the first place.

Some of the med students grumble about drinking an herbal tea, but a stern look from Jim is all the convincing they need. Soon all of the healthy people have had a dose. Day after day, you collect herbs and brew your tea. As you get better at finding the ingredients you need, you can make more and more. Soon you're able to brew enough that everyone in the village gets a dose every day or two.

Turn the page

The tea doesn't seem to help the sick very much. You and Tara cry together on the day that Maria finally loses her battle with the fever. Others follow. But amazingly, the number of sick all but stops growing. Over the next week, only three new cases come in.

In time, it becomes clear that you've discovered something really important. "We've got to get the word out before it's too late," Tara says. Jim heads into Port au Prince to show people how to brew the tea. Meanwhile, you and several others take the treatment from village to village.

Weeks go by. Months. On a supply run, Jim comes across an old long-range radio. You gather around with Jim, Tara, and some of the others as he tunes in to a radio broadcast from Miami.

Turn the page

" … as the fever spreads, more and more governments are falling into chaos. Madrid lies in ruin. Los Angeles has been evacuated. China has sealed its borders. Yet there seem to be slivers of hope. New anti-viral medications are showing promise. And an explosion of herbal remedies, said to have originated out of Haitian herbal lore, have been proven effective in preventing the disease among the healthy."

Tara smiles at you. The world will never be the same. You may never see your home again. But you're among people you love here. You don't know what will happen. But you're confident that humanity will survive, and you like to think that you played some small part in the battle against Blood Fever.

THE END

To follow another path, turn to page 10.
To learn more about virus outbreaks, turn to page 103.

"There's no time to waste," you tell Tara as you bring your brew to the hospital. The first patient you go to is Maria. She's awake, but just barely. Tara holds her head up as you carefully pour the tea into her mouth.

You go from patient to patient. Some of them grimace as they drink the bitter brew. One older man smiles weakly at you and says, "Merci!"

The pattern begins. By morning, you go out to collect the herbs you need. You brew the tea in the afternoon and bring it to the sick, but only after tasting it yourself to make sure it's right. At first, it seems to help. But the number of sick just keeps growing and growing. Within a week, the hospital is overflowing.

As you return from your herb collecting, you see Jim sitting with his head in his hands. You know he's got bad news.

Turn the page

"Maria passed on this morning," he tells you. But the news only gets worse from there. "And now Tara is sick. Most of the other medical students too."

Your heart sinks, but you knew this could happen. You rush to brew some tea and bring Tara the first cup.

Within days, the dead are mounting too quickly to bury. The healthy drag the bodies far from the village, lay them onto huge pyres and light them on fire.

On the day Tara dies, the rattle of an old motorcycle comes down the road. The village is almost deserted. You and Jim are the only healthy people left. You stay close as the rider approaches and removes his helmet.

From a distance, you exchange news. The rider, who speaks English, paints a dismal picture. "Port au Prince is all but wiped out. All of the major cities lie in ruin. The fever has spread globally. America, Europe, Africa, Asia, Australia. It's everywhere, mutating rapidly. Rumors say that the Chinese are close to a cure. But who knows?"

You can offer little news in return. You offer him a pouch loaded with herbs. "Jim and I have been taking these, and we haven't gotten sick yet," you explain. "I don't know if they're the reason, but it's worth a shot."

And just like that, the man is off. You have a terrible feeling in the pit of your stomach that he's the last healthy person you and Jim will see for a very, very long time. The plague has all but wiped out civilization. You can only hope there are enough other survivors for the human race to rise once again.

THE END

To follow another path, turn to page 10.
To learn more about virus outbreaks, turn to page 103.

The fever really kicks in the next day. Tara sets you up in a bed inside the hospital. "We're going to beat this," she says. "I had Peter make some calls to get you airlifted out of here."

But no help ever comes. You overhear a few of the students talking late that afternoon.

" … cases in Mexico, Cuba, Western Europe and Africa. Early reports of the fever spreading in Miami and New York City. Just about every nation has sealed its borders. There's nowhere to run."

The disease takes hold fast. You've always been healthy and strong, but your body has no defense for this virus. Still, at first, you fare better than most. You watch as patients around you grow sicker. The death toll reaches 25, then 40. When the wind is right, you can smell the smoke from the fires—the terrible fires where the dead are burned. That evening, Tara sits by your bedside. She's wearing her mask and gloves, but you still feel terrified that you'll infect her.

"I miss home," you tell her. Even the effort of speaking is exhausting. You've been having delusions, imagining that you see your friends from home in the room. Once, you could have sworn you spoke to a doctor from your mom's favorite TV show.

"I know," she answers. Her voice quivers. "We'll keep fighting. There's a village not far from here where nobody is sick. There might be something there worth checking out. Peter and I are the only ones still healthy, so I have to go, first thing in the morning."

You nod. It's all the energy you can spare.

"So I won't see you in the morning. I just wanted to … to see you before I go." She doesn't say, "to tell you good-bye," but you know that's what she means.

"I love you," she says, squeezing your hand.

It's your last memory before falling into a sleep from which you'll never awake.

THE END

To follow another path, turn to page 10.
To learn more about virus outbreaks, turn to page 103.

You don't like this. Not a bit. "Jim! Run!" you shout, opening your door and bolting toward the road. You run as fast as your feet can carry you, but the sound of another gunshot stops you in your tracks.

You turn in time to see Jim slump to the ground. One of the young men holds a sawed-off shotgun, and he's staring right at you. There's nothing you can do for Jim. All you can do is run.

You run until you can't run anymore. You don't care where you're going, just as long as it's away from that gang. Finally, you slump to the ground next to an old concrete building that sits on a terraced slope overlooking the Gulf of Gonâve. The building is cracked and abandoned—probably a victim of the terrible earthquake that struck Haiti in 2010. But that means nobody is around, and right now, that's a good thing.

Turn the page

The sea looks so peaceful. But the scene around you is far from it. Smoke rises from dozens of fires scattered around the city. In the distance, you can hear gunfire. The streets are all but deserted. Those who haven't caught the fever have shut themselves in.

That's when it hits you. You're lost and alone in a city crumbling from a plague unlike anything the modern world has ever encountered. You have no food, water, or money. You have no way back to Tara, much less back home. Even if you survive the streets and find food and water, you won't survive the plague. Not if you stay here.

You stare out at the ocean and it hits you. *The marina.* Your grandfather taught you a little about sailing. You stand up, brush yourself off, and head toward the marina. The few people you encounter along the way steer clear of you.

Most of the boats you see are far too big for you to handle alone. But there, tucked away near the shore, you spot it. A laser-style boat—small and perfect for a single sailor. You climb aboard, cut the boat free, and head for open water as quickly as you can. The sooner you're out of Port au Prince and away from civilization, the better.

The waves lap against the hull of your boat as the city grows smaller in the distance. You scan the horizon. The Caribbean is filled with small islands and atolls. Maybe, just maybe, you can find somewhere safe to wait out the outbreak. It won't be easy, but you've escaped Haiti already. You have to believe that you'll be resourceful enough to overcome the obstacles ahead.

THE END

To follow another path, turn to page 10.
To learn more about virus outbreaks, turn to page 103.

Jim's probably right. They're looking for supplies, and your Jeep makes a perfect target. You crane your neck to watch as Jim steps from the Jeep and raises his hands above his head. He shouts something in French.

The gunshot that rings out is deafening. At first, you hardly believe what you're seeing. Jim slumps to the ground. The gang, at least a dozen young men, is on you. You scream and lunge to lock the driver's side door, but you're not quick enough. One of the young men, his face glistening in sweat and covered in fever blisters, throws the door open.

You scream again and kick as the men drag you from the car. You desperately try to break free but have no success. You bite and claw as they throw you roughly to the ground. You refuse to flinch when one of them levels a sawed-off shotgun at your head. You should have run when you had the chance.

THE END
To follow another path, turn to page 10.
To learn more about virus outbreaks, turn to page 103.

"The villagers need you here," you tell Tara, holding her arm. "With Jim gone, the hospital is already short-handed. They can't spare you too. I can run into the city, see if there's any sign of Jim's Jeep. Just tell me where he usually goes for supplies. I can be gone and back before sundown."

Tara shakes her head. "No, you're too young to go."

"Don't be ridiculous. This is an emergency. I know how to ride and I'll be careful."

Tara finally gives in. You pack a backpack and climb onto the rusty old motorcycle. Soon you're rumbling down an all but deserted highway.

As you ride into Port au Prince, the gravity of the situation hits you. The city lies in ruin. Fires burn everywhere. A haze of smoke hangs over the city. You pull a shirt from your backpack and wrap it around your face.

You glance at the crude map Tara drew for you. There's a supermarket half a mile off the highway. But as you take the exit, you see several cars blocking the road. It isn't until you're right beside them that you realize that one of them is Jim's Jeep. It's completely gutted. What looters didn't take, the fire destroyed. You shiver as you see a series of holes—bullet holes—on the driver's side door.

"Jim!" you shout. But you know it's useless. If he's okay, he'd be long gone by now.

There's nothing more for you here. You start to turn the motorcycle around to head back when you hear a man shout out. You don't need much French to know that you're being ordered to stop.

The voice comes from behind you. You spin and see two men. One holds a shotgun, and it's aimed right at you.

Turn the page

The other man steps forward and forces you from the motorcycle. He's covered in blood blisters, and beads of sweat run down his face. He sneers at you, then sneezes. Disgusted and scared, you turn and run.

The streets of Port au Prince are filthy. Dead bodies lie scattered along the roads. Feral dogs roam from abandoned building to abandoned building. You chase them out of a burned-out tin shack and slump to the ground.

You're stuck here. You speak little French, have no money, and can't make it back to Tara. And based on what you've seen at the camp, you'll start showing symptoms of Blood Fever as soon as tomorrow.

You drop your head into your hands and sob. One thought keeps repeating in your head: *Why didn't I just go home?*

THE END
To follow another path, turn to page 10.
To learn more about virus outbreaks, turn to page 103.

From everything you've read, the virus is no laughing matter. It would be foolish for you to stay here knowing you could catch it. With a sigh, you agree to turn around and go back home.

After a long, disappointing flight and a restless night's sleep, you're back to your routine at home. You catch the latest sci-fi thriller at the mall with your friends, you spend an afternoon mini golfing, and you dig into a new novel. Life seems perfectly normal.

Yet the news tells a different story in the Caribbean. One evening after supper, the TV shows images from the Dominican Republic. Field hospitals are overflowing. You watch the crawl at the bottom of the screen:

More than 300 dead in the Dominican Republic ... Outbreaks in Haiti, Puerto Rico, Cuba reaching critical levels ... World Health Organization describes virus as "alarming" ... Recent scares in Miami, Houston, and Madrid have millions fleeing the cities ...

Turn the page

By Tuesday—just four days after your return—the news is plastered with stories of Blood Fever in North America, Europe, and Northern Africa. News anchors and reporters seem really worried. The virus is spreading at rates never before seen.

A week later, you're home alone when you hear the sirens. As you head outside to check it out, the phone rings. It's your dad. He and your mom were visiting your aunt, and you know from his tone that the news is bad. "We're stuck in traffic," he says. "Nothing is moving. There are emergency vehicles everywhere. It's Blood Fever. It's here. We'll be home as soon as we can. Until then, stay inside."

Your mind is racing. What are you supposed to do? You've seen enough disaster movies to know that food and water are always the first priority. Maybe it would be smart to stock up before things get out of hand. Or maybe the best idea is to lock the doors and keep away from people.

To stay at home, turn to page 64.
To go on a supply run, turn to page 66.

Everything you've heard about Blood Fever says that it's more contagious than anything people have ever seen. You shut the windows, lock the doors, and plop down onto the couch. An hour passes, then two. Finally, the phone rings again.

"Sorry, kiddo," says your dad. "I don't think we're going to make it home. They're shutting down the highway. Gonna grab a motel room tonight and try again tomorrow."

Alone and growing more frightened by the moment, you decide to watch the news. It's almost impossible to believe. More than 100,000 dead already, and that number is growing so fast that nobody seems to know what's going to happen. The governments of the Dominican Republic and Haiti are in full collapse. Much of Miami is in flames, and people are fleeing cities everywhere.

And it's no longer happening just on your TV screen. Sirens echo through the night. No one is out on the streets. You try to call your dad the next morning, but all the lines are busy.

Another day passes with no word from your parents. You're terrified to leave the house. You don't speak to a single soul. Huge clouds of thick black smoke climb into the sky. The water from the tap stops flowing, and the lights flicker for several moments. Perhaps most frightening of all, you no longer hear any sirens. You're feeling depressed and scared as you click off the TV and climb into bed.

That night the sound of shattering glass wakes you from your shallow sleep. You sit up, hands shaking. Then you hear footsteps and voices. "Take it," rasps a man's voice. "Everything you can find. Take it all." You're being robbed!

To hide, turn to page 68.
To confront the people robbing your house,
turn to page 89.

You ride your bike to a grocery store a few blocks away. The place is swamped with people. A huge spray-painted sign out front reads: "NO HOARDING PLEASE!" But people seem to be ignoring it. One woman rushes past you pushing a grocery cart filled with bottled water and canned goods. She looks at you and slows down.

"Go now," she tells you. "There's not much left, and people are starting to become aggressive. Take anything you can get!"

With that, she runs to her car with the cart. People are streaming in and out of the store, carrying all kinds of boxes, bottles, bags. You wonder if there can be much left at all.

That's when you hear the gunfire, followed by screaming. The situation is going downhill fast. People are panicking. You've got to act now.

To risk going inside the grocery store to get supplies,
turn to page 71.
To try your luck somewhere else, turn to page 75.

Carefully, you slip out of bed, tiptoe across your bedroom floor, and crawl into the back of your closet. You listen to the clanging sounds from below and shiver with fear. Everything is going wrong so fast!

The minutes drag on until all you hear is your own rapid breathing. Finally, you feel safe enough to climb out and creep downstairs. It's silent—they're gone.

You groan as you look at the kitchen. Shattered glass and plates litter the floor. The refrigerator and cupboards are empty, and they took anything of value. You slump to the floor and put your head down.

That's when you hear shouting outside. You peer out the window and see flames licking the outer wall of the house next door! *Oh no! Mrs. Thomas!*

Mrs. Thomas is 85 years old and lives alone in that house. The flames climb up the outer walls and rise along the roof line. Your houses are only a dozen feet apart. The blaze is sure to spread to your house!

To gather everything you can from your own house
before the fire spreads, turn to page 72.
To rush to help Mrs. Thomas, turn to page 83.

It's now or never. You park your bike and shove your way inside. You're shocked by what you see. People are scooping up handfuls of groceries and running out of the store. You see two women fighting over a cart. Several employees are trying to maintain order, but the hoarding has turned into looting.

The cereal aisle lies in front of you. The shelves have been ransacked. Open cereal boxes lie everywhere. Spilled cereal crunches beneath your feet. You spot a bag of granola under some trash and grab it.

Over the next several chaotic minutes, you manage to grab several cans of beans, some tomato soup, and a jar of peanuts. You carry it all in a cloth shopping bag. The chaos is growing worse by the moment. It's time to get out while you still can.

To get out now without paying, turn to page 74.
To attempt to pay for your groceries, turn to page 87.

For all you know, Mrs. Thomas isn't even home. It would be foolish to rush next door.

Your mind races. You know you only have minutes to grab what you can. You rush into your room, throw open your top drawer, and grab the envelope full of cash that you've collected. You shove it into your backpack, along with some clothes, a hunting knife your dad gave you, a family photo, and a spare T-shirt that you can wrap around your face as a mask. You're zipping up the pack when the house's smoke detectors begin their shrill screaming. Time's up!

You throw your pack over your shoulder and dart into the hallway. Already the smoke is thickening. You bound down the stairs, out the door, and onto the street. As you move, you see three dark figures in the distance.

No time to stick around. You slide around the side of the house to where you park your bike, climb on, and begin to pedal as fast as you can. Only when you're miles away do you stop to catch your breath.

What are you supposed to do now? Your home is gone. The town has fallen into chaos. Half the people are sick and dying. And many others seem to have gone crazy. Is anyplace safe? Your aunt and uncle live about 30 miles away. But is there any reason to believe the situation there is better? Would you be best off just finding somewhere far from people and waiting out the crisis?

To head toward your aunt and uncle's house,
turn to page 80.
To find somewhere in the woods to wait out the crisis,
turn to page 98.

You don't believe in stealing. But as you scan the store, you realize that nobody is there to even take your money. The only clerk you can see appears busy cramming supplies into her own bag! You'd seen images of looting on the news. But you never thought it would happen *here*! It's time to leave before looting turns into full-scale rioting. You breathe a sigh of relief as you step outside and climb on your bike.

Your mind races as you pedal your bike away from the store. You can hardly believe that this is happening in your own hometown! People are panicking, and everything is starting to break down. Blood Fever is bad, but it seems at this point that the panic might be even worse.

Lost in your thoughts, it takes a few minutes before you notice the rising smoke. You're only blocks from your home when you see it. The blaze covers your entire block! Several people are running from the scene. You recognize a neighbor, crying, clinging to a photo album.

Turn the page

By the time firefighters arrive, it's too late. At least seven homes have been completely destroyed—including your own. Smoke rises in several other parts of the city. You hear distant sirens.

The days that follow are a blur. At first, you're brought to a makeshift shelter at your high school's gym. But one night there is too much. People everywhere, coughing, sneezing. Staying there seems like a death sentence. You try a friend's house, but no one answers when you knock. You spend the night alone in your friend's tree house.

Turn the page

Meanwhile, the situation gets worse by the hour. The bodies of the dead pile up in the streets. Even worse is the smell of the bonfires where people are burning the bodies. In a matter of weeks, your nice, modern town has fallen into what feels like the Dark Ages.

You keep your distance from people as best you can. It's not hard to do. Nobody seems to want to get close. What few conversations you do have are shouted from a distance. The rumor is that the army has set up a refugee camp several towns over. You've still got your bike—the only real possession you have. You can't keep living on the street, so you begin the journey.

About halfway there, you spot another kid about your age on a motorized scooter. From across the street, you greet each other.

"Hey there," he calls. "You're healthy, right?" You nod. "Thought so. I can spot a sick one a mile away. My name's Nate. Me and some other kids have a spot out of town. It's just an old abandoned country church. But we're all healthy, and we're working together to get through this. I think you'd fit right in. Do you want to join us?"

To join Nate's group, turn to page 90.
To continue to the refugee camp, turn to page 96.

It's clear that your parents aren't coming home. You don't know if they're alive or dead. You're a teenager in a world gone mad. What you need is family. You tug the straps of your backpack tight and begin the long ride.

It's an eerie midnight ride. The streets are deserted. Even the highway stands dark. Yet as you ride past homes and boarded-up businesses, you hear the occasional distant scream. At one point, you watch as several helicopters speed overhead. They look military, but it's hard to be sure in the dark.

Dawn is breaking when you arrive at the bridge that leads into your aunt and uncle's town. You hear shouting in the distance. As you pedal, you see a huge crowd of people spilling into the street. People are screaming, throwing things. A teenage boy rides a motorized scooter in your direction. "You sick?" he shouts. You shake your head.

Turn the page

"Don't go that way then. It's a hot zone. Everyone there'll be dead in a week."

"What about you?" you ask.

"Not sick. Not yet, at least. On a supply run, but I'll have to look somewhere else."

The boy, Nate, is in a camp out of town with a dozen other kids. They were part of a scouting group when the plague struck. Now they're living in an abandoned country church. "You'd fit in just fine." he says, looking you up and down and seeing no signs of illness. "Care to join us?"

To follow Nate, turn to page 90.
To take your chances in town, turn to page 93.

You sprint down the stairs and through the doorway. You leap over the hedges and throw open the door to Mrs. Thomas' house. Smoke pours out of the doorway.

"Mrs. Thomas!" you shout, pulling your shirt up to cover your mouth and nose. "Are you in here?"

"Help me!" you hear. It's coming from the kitchen. You rush inside, squinting because the smoke stings your eyes. Mrs. Thomas is lying on the floor. There's blood on her face, and she's coughing violently.

"Come on, we gotta get you out of here!" The woman groans with pain as you help her to her feet. She leans against you as you help her out of the house. You move her across the street, away from the fire, until you both collapse onto a neighbor's lawn.

"Help us!" you shout. You're afraid Mrs. Thomas might not make it. Just then you see a military jeep rumbling down the road.

Turn the page

"You!" shouts a man dressed in a military uniform. You can't see his face, as it's covered by an elaborate mask. "We saw the flames. Is everyone all right?"

"Yes. I think so," you tell the man, an Army captain named Taylor. A medic takes a blood sample from you and places it inside a test unit. As he waits, the medic examines Mrs. Thomas. "She's in bad shape," says the medic. "She would recover from her injuries. But … she's got it. She's infected. Take her to Holding Camp 7."

"What does that mean, captain?" you ask, panic creeping into your voice.

Captain Taylor gives you a sad look. "She's going to a camp for the infected," he answers. At that moment, the little testing unit beeps. A green light blinks on the display.

"Your sample is clean. You're not infected. So you're heading north, to the mountains. The virus doesn't seem to like high altitude. We're moving people there while our scientists work on a cure."

Turn the page

You feel a sense of relief wash over you. "Hold on a second, captain," says the medic before turning to you. "Did you just carry this woman out of her burning house?"

You nod. Behind you, you can hear Mrs. Thomas' hacking cough.

The medic looks to Captain Taylor and shakes his head. Your heart sinks as it hits you. Mrs. Thomas is infected. You carried her, coughing and bleeding, out of her house. That means you're infected now too.

The captain gives you a long, sad look. "Sorry, kid. Was a heroic thing you did there. Wish there was something I could do." He turns and shouts. "We've got two infected for transport!"

And with that, you're off to a camp for the infected. You know that without a miracle, it's where you'll spend the final days of your life.

THE END

To follow another path, turn to page 10.
To learn more about virus outbreaks, turn to page 103.

Just because others are stealing, that doesn't make it right. With your bag in hand, you stride up to the customer service counter, where a woman is frantically trying to telephone for help.

"Can I pay for this here?" you shout.

The woman gives you a strange look, like she doesn't quite believe what you're asking. Just then, a young man steps up behind you. "Please," he says, coughing into his sleeve. "I need help. I've got two little ones at home, and someone broke in and took all of our food!" The clerk barely seems to notice. She's grabbing supplies from behind the counter.

The man grasps your shoulder. "Help me! Please!" A shiver traces your spine as you look at the man. His face is covered in blisters. His hands feel warm through the material of your T-shirt. You back away, thrusting the bag at the man. "Take it," you shout, willing to do anything to get away from him. You run out of the store and pedal home as fast as you can.

Turn the page

The symptoms begin two days later. You're on the couch, shivering, clutching a bucket in case you need to vomit. You try to follow the news on the TV, but your attention wanders. Entire cities are burning. Governments are collapsing all around the world. There's talk of an experimental treatment, but nobody seems to have any details.

Desperate, you climb on your bike and start riding toward the hospital. You have to stop once to throw up in a bush, but you somehow manage to make it. Sadly, you find no help there. Hundreds of people crowd around the building. There isn't a bed to be found. One elderly man explains to you that most of the doctors have fallen ill themselves.

It was your last hope. You look around and see death everywhere. You know that without a miracle, that will be your fate as well.

THE END

To follow another path, turn to page 10.
To learn more about virus outbreaks, turn to page 103.

Someone in your house stealing your food and supplies? Your blood boils at the thought. You scan your room for a weapon. Propped against the wall is a baseball bat—perfect.

Clutching the aluminum bat, you creep down the hallway. You hear two voices and crashing noises as the burglars pull things out of your cabinets. Rounding the corner into the kitchen, you raise the bat above your head and shout "STOP!"

Two men, dressed all in black, are loading canned food into a large grain bag. For a moment, they look shocked. But that soon passes.

"Put the bag down and get out of my house," you stammer. You try your hardest to sound strong, but your voice wavers and cracks.

"Bad move, kid," says one of the man as he pulls a pistol from his waistband. You don't even have time to swing your bat before he pulls the trigger.

THE END
To follow another path, turn to page 10.
To learn more about virus outbreaks, turn to page 103.

You have nowhere to go. It's an easy decision. You angle your bike around and follow Nate out of town, turning off on a small dirt road that's little more than two ruts in the countryside. After a few miles, he points out the abandoned church.

"It's not much to look at, but it keeps the rain and wind off of us."

There are 12 other kids there, all about your age. Some carry water from a nearby well. Others collect wood for the fire. One girl is butchering a rabbit.

"We figure things are gonna get worse before they get better," Nate says, introducing you to the others as you pass by. Most seem friendly, once they're assured that you're not sick. "We'll wait it out, relying on each other to get through it. Strength in numbers, you know."

Turn the page

And so the group becomes your new family. Over the next several months, you live and work together, keeping away from the rest of civilization as much as you can. You help operate the group's long-range radio, monitoring the news as best you can.

The world is falling apart. According to the radio, as many as 95 percent of the world's people are dead. But as the months crawl by, Blood Fever wanes. The survivors have finally developed an immunity to the virus. Soon it will be time to leave your safe home and rebuild. It will be a long and painful process, but you're just grateful that you're alive to have the chance. Someday, you'll set out to search for your parents and friends. But for now, you're safe.

THE END
To follow another path, turn to page 10.
To learn more about virus outbreaks, turn to page 103.

"I need to find my aunt and uncle," you tell the boy, waving as you begin to pedal. He gives you a disappointed look, shrugs his shoulders, and heads the other way.

The streets are madness. You try to slip by quietly, but to no avail. Several people turn toward you. You hear a woman's voice shout, "A bike! Get it!"

You turn and try to pedal hard. But something slams into your bike from behind. Your rear tire skids on the pavement. You react quickly to right your balance, but then someone is grabbing you. More hands pull you down. "No! Leave me alone! Stop!" you cry. But no one is listening.

The rush is on. People are fighting and clawing at each other, trying to get your bike. A man grabs your backpack from your shoulder, yanking it so hard that the strap snaps. You reach out and grab at the other strap, but the man turns and kicks you hard in the shoulder. Your arm goes numb from the pain and drops to the pavement.

Turn the page

In time, the mob moves on. You lie on the street, bleeding and in pain. Your shoulder is either badly sprained or broken, and you can't put weight on one of your ankles. Worse still, everything you owned is gone.

An old woman stands over you. "You weren't sick?" she says. You shake your head. She gives you a sad look. "You are now. Sorry, child."

You know she's right. Blood Fever is so contagious that just being near a sick person is likely to get you infected. And you just faced a mob.

You'll be feeling the first symptoms soon. You know that there's nowhere you can go for help. If your aunt and uncle aren't sick already, you can't expose them. You wish you'd stayed with Tara. At least there, you'd have been with family.

THE END
To follow another path, turn to page 10.
To learn more about virus outbreaks, turn to page 103.

You don't know this kid, and you're not about to trust a stranger with your life. "Thanks for the offer. I've got somewhere to be."

Nate shrugs, then he's off. You ride through the day and into the night. By the time you see the camp in the distance, you're hungry, dehydrated, and exhausted.

The camp sits behind a tall chain-link fence. You approach the gate, guarded by trio of armed military police. "I need help," you tell them.

They look you over, then look at each other. "Sick," one of them whispers.

"No! I'm not sick, I swear it." You realize how you must look. You're thin from eating poorly, pale from lack of sleep and water. Your hair is matted, and your face is dirty. You're drenched in sweat from the long ride.

"Okay, sure thing, kid," says one of the MPs, backing away. "We'll get you set up in a nice spot right away."

The MP straps on a mask and leads you inside. Immediately you're led inside a building, down a flight of stairs, and through an underground tunnel. Men and women wearing bright yellow biohazard suits come and go.

"They'll take care of you in here," says the MP, leading you into a room filled with cots. There, dozens of people lie, coughing, vomiting … dying. You spin and shout "No!" as the heavy metal door locks shut behind you.

An intercom sounds. "Please select a cot. A medic will be with you shortly."

You slump to the floor. You weren't infected, but now you certainly are. And you know that means you'll never be leaving.

THE END
To follow another path, turn to page 10.
To learn more about virus outbreaks, turn to page 103.

Being around people isn't safe. Even the healthy people are a danger now. That means you've only got one option. You tighten the straps on your pack and begin to ride. You've already got a spot in mind. Your parents take you camping sometimes in a nearby national park. If they're still alive and healthy, maybe they'll find you there. It's a long shot, but you'll take it.

You get there just before dawn. It's deserted. The reflection of the sunrise on the smooth water almost makes you forget the madness you just left behind.

A week passes. You're grateful for the outdoors skills your parents taught you. You've made yourself a crude shelter, built a fire pit, collected and boiled drinking water, and even caught some fish. If not for the dark plumes of smoke in the distant sky, you might imagine it was all a bad dream.

Turn the page

Another week goes by. You can't stand not knowing. So you hike down to the trailhead, near where you hid your bike. There's a small town a few miles up the road.

As you pedal your bike into town, you know things are still very wrong. The streets appear empty. Doors and windows are boarded up. It feels like a ghost town.

That's when the shot rings out. The bullet clangs off a metal mailbox not 10 feet from where you're standing.

"Don't want no trouble!" shouts a voice. It's a woman. You can see her in the window of one of the buildings that lines the street.

"I'm not sick!" you shout back, holding your arms out to your side.

"Don't care. Just head back out the way you came. Like I said, we don't want trouble. But I'll shoot you if I have to."

You don't have much choice. You back away, climb back onto your bike, and pedal back.

That night, in front of your campfire, you smile. That didn't go well. But now you know people are surviving. The virus will run its course. You're sure of that. And then it will be time to rebuild. All you have to do is keep yourself alive until then. It will be a long, difficult process, but you're certain you can do it.

You reflect as you stare into the dancing flames of your fire. You've lost so much—your home, your family, your friends. But you're alive and healthy. You have a chance, and you won't let it slip away.

THE END

To follow another path, turn to page 10.
To learn more about virus outbreaks, turn to page 103.

THREATS FROM WITHIN:
PANDEMICS OF PAST AND PRESENT

Smallpox, the Spanish flu, Ebola, the Black Death. The only things scarier than the names are the diseases themselves. Blood Fever isn't real, but throughout history, people have waged an unending battle with diseases. Many illnesses, such as the common cold, aren't much more than a nuisance to otherwise healthy people.

But once in awhile, a disease pops up that wreaks havoc on the human body. These diseases can kill and spread at alarming rates. Entire cities, countries, and continents can be affected. This is a pandemic, or plague.

For many, the word *plague* brings to mind one of the most deadly diseases known to humans. The Black Death, or Bubonic Plague, struck Europe during the 1300s. Nobody knows exactly when it began or where it came from.

The bacteria that caused the Black Death killed as many as 75 million people. Historians estimate that the Black Death killed between one-third and two-thirds of Europe's entire population. It brought Western civilization to the brink of collapse.

In the late 1400s and early 1500s, Europeans sailed across the Atlantic Ocean to North America. They brought with them many diseases, such as measles, smallpox, and scarlet fever. Europeans had developed immunity to these diseases. Their bodies knew how to battle them. But the Native Americans had no such defenses. The diseases ripped through native populations, wiping out entire nations. Experts estimate that as many as 20 million Native Americans died, mainly from smallpox. That figure may have represented 95 percent of the native population!

Recent outbreaks such as AIDS, swine flu, and Ebola prove that plagues are not just a thing of the past. Many people remain confident that modern medicine and science can fend off most diseases.

Others aren't convinced. Diseases have shown they can adapt to even the most potent medicines. Many bacterial diseases were once easily cured with antibiotics. But over time, the bacteria mutated. The diseases have become resistant to drugs. It's proof that the battle between medicine and disease is ongoing and, perhaps, neverending.

It's not just mutated diseases that are the problem. New threats of disease—both natural and those created in human laboratories—are always arising. Today a person can travel halfway across the globe in a day. That gives diseases the chance to spread at rates impossible in ancient times. What would happen if a new deadly disease spread so quickly that even modern medicine could not keep up? Could such a devastating plague threaten civilization, and even humanity itself? Agencies such as the World Health Organization (WHO) and the U.S. Centers for Disease Control (CDC) work to keep the threat to a minimum.

SURVIVAL REFERENCE GUIDE

If a terrible virus ever threatened to wipe out humanity, you'd need every advantage to survive. In this story, there was little warning. But in real life, we might have weeks or even months to prepare before the worst of the plague. What sort of items might you gather to maximize your chances of survival? Here's a survival pack! Stock up—you might have to stay away from other people for a long time!

SURVIVAL KIT

*A breathing mask or surgical mask

*Hand sanitizer

*Disinfectants such as rubbing alcohol

*A first-aid kit with lots of sterile bandages

*A battery-operated short-wave radio with plenty of batteries

*A small power generator or solar panels

*A year's supply of any prescription medication you need, such as asthma inhalers

*Reference books and survival guides (the Internet may not be available)

*Flashlights

*Canned or dehydrated food

*Bottled water and water purification tablets

*A few good books—you may be spending a lot of time alone!

TEN THINGS TO REMEMBER DURING A PANDEMIC

- **Don't shake hands.** It might seem rude, but a handshake is like public transit for a virus. Go with a polite nod and wave instead.

- **Hospitals aren't really sterile.** Hospitals might seem like super-clean, sterile places. But they're really crawling with germs. Head to the hospital only when you really need to.

- **One may be the loneliest number, but it's also the safest.** People are social creatures. We crave the company of others. But during an outbreak, isolation is your safest bet. Keep your contact with others to a bare minimum. You can't avoid your family, but you can sure steer clear of the mall!

- **Be informed.** That means reading newspapers, Internet news portals, and watching the news on TV. Pay attention to what's going on. There's no substitute for knowledge.

- **Wash, wash, and wash some more**. Your number one defense against infection? Clean hands. Every time you touch a doorknob, light switch, or anything in public, you're risking getting viruses or bacteria on your hands. From there, it's a short trip to your mouth, nose, or eyes. Wash frequently. Use soap and hand sanitizer.

- **Cover your sneezes and coughs.** If you are sick, a cough or sneeze can be like a virus-spewing bomb. Sneeze into your sleeve and keep your germs to yourself!

- **Looks can be deceiving.** People don't appear sick the moment they catch a virus. It usually takes a couple of days. Just because someone *looks* healthy doesn't mean they aren't infected!

- **Stock up.** As soon as a pandemic starts, stock up on essentials. Every trip to the store is a risk. If you've got supplies for a week or two, you can stay safely locked away in your own home.

- **Know the warning signs.** Most diseases have telltale signs. Whether it's coughing, sneezing, fever, or blisters, know the early signs of an infection. Early treatment can be the difference between life and death!

- **Desperate people do desperate things.** Most people in the world are basically good and well-intentioned. But when push comes to shove, they look out first for themselves and their families. During an outbreak, you might have to set your trusting nature on the back burner.

GLOSSARY

ANTI-VIRAL (an-ti-VYE-ruhl)—a medicine that helps the body fight off viral infections

CONTAGIOUS (kun-TAY-juss)—easily spread and having a high rate of infection

DEHYDRATED (dee-HY-dray-tuhd)—lacking water in the body

DELUSION (di-LOO-zhuhn)—a false vision or experience; people having delusions may think they see people or things that aren't really there

HOARD (HORD)—to stockpile valuable supplies

IMMUNITY (i-MYOO-nuh-tee)—a body's natural defense against a disease

INFECT (in-FEKT)—to cause someone to catch a disease

LOOT (LOOT)—to steal from stores or houses during a war or other disaster

MUTATE (MYOO-tayt)—to change in form; as viruses mutate, they can become more difficult to treat

PANDEMIC (pan-DEM-ik)—an outbreak of a disease that infects large numbers of people worldwide

PLAGUE (PLAYG)—an uncontrolled outbreak of a deadly disease

PYRE (PYE-er)—a large pile of wood or other burnable material often used for burning dead bodies

STERILE (STER-uhl)—clean and free of microorganisms such as bacteria

VACCINATE (VAK-suh-nayt)—to protect someone against disease by introducing his or her immune system to a dead or dormant virus or bacteria

READ MORE

Love, Ann, and Jane Drake. *Pandemic Survival: It's Why You're Alive.* Toronto, Ontario: Tundra Books, 2013.

Stille, Darlene R. *Outbreak!: The Science of Pandemics.* North Mankato, Minn.: Compass Point Books, 2011.

INTERNET SITES

Use FactHound to find Internet sites related to this book. All of the sites on FactHound have been researched by our staff.

Here's all you do:
Visit *www.facthound.com*
Type in this code: 9781491458518

AUTHOR

Matt Doeden is the author of more than 200 children's fiction and non-fiction books. A lifelong fan of science fiction and "what if" stories, he lives in Minnesota with his wife and two children.

ILLUSTRATOR

A native of Yorkshire (England), Stewart Johnson began freelancing in 1986. He originally started illustrating for the UK RPG market before moving into the comics market. He began working for British publishers Fleetway and Marvel UK. He left the comics field for two years for advertising before returning in 1993 to work for American publishers DC Comics & Marvel Comics. He is married with two daughters.